RACCOONS

Jen Green

Grolier
an imprint of

 SCHOLASTIC

www.scholastic.com/librarypublishing

Published 2008 by Grolier
An imprint of Scholastic Library Publishing
Old Sherman Turnpike, Danbury,
Connecticut 06816

For The Brown Reference Group plc
Project Editor: Jolyon Goddard
Copy-editors: Lisa Hughes, Tom Jackson
Picture Researcher: Clare Newman
Designers: Jeni Child, Lynne Ross,
    Sarah Williams
Managing Editor: Bridget Giles

Volume ISBN-13: 978-0-7172-6281-6
Volume ISBN-10: 0-7172-6281-2

**Library of Congress
Cataloging-in-Publication Data**

Nature's children. Set 3.
    p. cm.
Includes bibliographical references and
index.
ISBN 13: 978-0-7172-8082-7
ISBN 10: 0-7172-8082-9
1. Animals--Encyclopedias, Juvenile. I.
Grolier Educational (Firm)
QL49.N384 2008
590.3--dc22
                    2007031568

Printed and bound in China

Contents

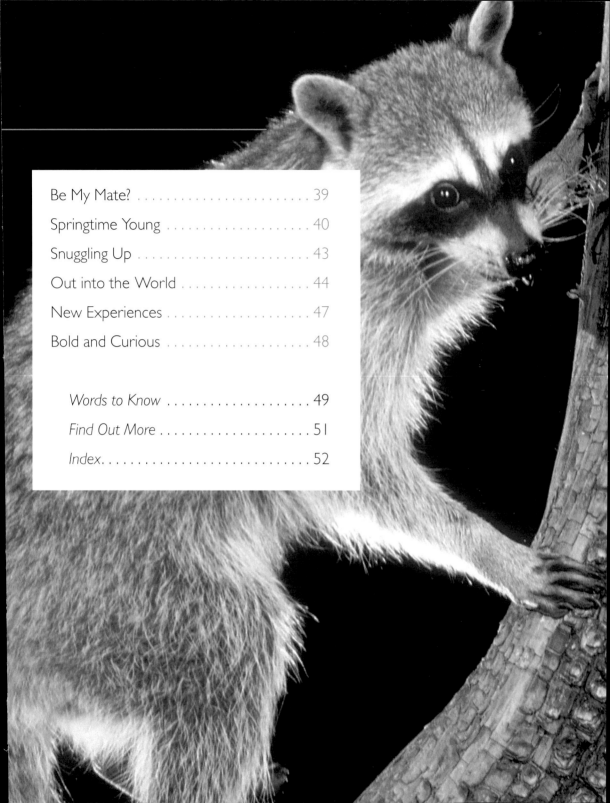

FACT FILE: Raccoons

Class	Mammals (Mammalia)
Order	Carnivores (Carnivora)
Family	Raccoon family (Procyonidae)
Genus	*Procyon*
Species	Common raccoon (*Procyon lotor*), crab-eating raccoon (*P. cancrivorous*), and Cozumel Island raccoon (*P. pygmaeus*)
World distribution	The common raccoon ranges from southern Canada to Central America; the crab-eating raccoon ranges from Costa Rica to northern Argentina; the Cozumel Island raccoon lives on Cozumel Island, Yucatán, Mexico
Habitat	Mainly woods and scrublands, preferably near water; also grasslands, farms, marshes, towns and cities, and on coasts
Distinctive physical characteristics	The common raccoon has grayish fur with a wide band of dark fur across the eyes and cheeks, a banded tail, a broad head with oval-shaped ears, and a pointed snout
Habits	Mostly live alone, except females with young; they are active at night; in northern areas, raccoons sleep much of the winter
Diet	Buds, small animals, fish, shellfish, fruit, nuts, and seeds

Introduction

Raccoons have a striped tail and a face that looks like a bandit's mask. They seem to have a bandit's thieving habits, too. Those that live near people go on nightly raids to steal food, from farms or even from garbage cans, which they tip over. They then make a getaway under the cover of darkness, long before the theft is discovered. There is more to raccoons than the mischief they cause, however. Raccoons are clever and playful animals, supremely suited to hunting at night. Female raccoons are excellent mothers, too.

A common raccoon searches for food in a garden.

The ringtailed coati lives in the forests of South America.

Raccoon Relatives

The raccoon family has 16 members. Only three of them are **species**, or types, of raccoons. The common, or North American, raccoon is widespread in the United States and Central America. The two less common species are the crab-eating raccoon from Central America and South America and the Cozumel Island raccoon from Cozumel Island, Yucatán, Mexico.

All but one of the other members of the raccoon family live in Central America and South America, or both. Many have a banded tail like the common raccoon, and some share its dark mask. These relatives are coatis, the kinkajou (KIHN-KAH-JOO), olingos, the ringtail, and the cacomistle (KAH-KOH-MIHS-UHL). The relative that lives outside the Americas is the red panda of the Himalayas and south China.

Raccoons are part of a bigger group of **mammals** called **carnivores**, or meat eaters. This large group includes cats, dogs, bears, stoats, and mongooses.

Raccoon Country

Common raccoons like to live in woodlands, particularly by water. They are also found by coasts. These flexible animals are able to make themselves comfortable in many kinds of habitats, including grasslands, dry scrublands, and on farms. They have also moved into cities and suburbs, where they make their home in sheds and garages, up trees, or inside drainpipes. In fact, you may well have raccoons living in your backyard! They don't like it too cold, however. For this reason, raccoons do not live in northern Canada or high up mountains.

An urban raccoon is always on the lookout for food.

By climbing
a tree stump,
this raccoon gets
a better view to
look for food.

10

Size and Shape

If you saw a raccoon from behind, you might mistake it for a house cat. However, raccoons are usually larger than even the plumpest house cat. Their head is broader than a cat's, with rounder ears and a much more pointed snout. Their body is rounder and their legs are shorter than a cat's, too.

Male raccoons usually measure about 22 inches (55 cm) from nose to rear. In addition, their tail is about 10 inches (25 cm) long. Adult male raccoons weigh about 18 pounds (8 kg). The females are a little smaller and lighter. Raccoons that live in northern areas, where the weather can get cold, are usually larger than raccoons that live in the south. The extra bulk helps them keep warm in cold weather.

Bundle of Fur

Grayish brown fur covers most of a common raccoon's body. This fur is really two coats in one. On top is a layer of long, smooth hairs called **guard hairs**. These black and gray hairs keep out the wind and rain. Below is a dense, brown woolly underfur. This keeps the raccoon very warm in winter. The underfur grows thicker in fall and is shed, or molted, in spring.

The raccoon's most obvious feature is its banditlike mask. The mask is made up of dark fur around each eye, extending down across each cheek. The raccoon also has a beautifully banded tail, with five to seven dark rings and a black tip. The raccoon's markings help to break up its outline. That makes it more difficult to see, especially at night, when it hunts. This natural disguise is called **camouflage**.

All three species
of raccoons have
a black eye mask.

13

The name *raccoon* comes from the Algonkian Native American word *arakun*, meaning "he who scratches with his hands."

14

Toes and Fingers

Raccoons have five toes on each of their front and hind feet. Their paw prints look a little like a human baby's hand- and footprints. However, a raccoon's paws are very different from a baby's hands and feet. The raccoon's toes are longer, and end in short claws. The best place to look for raccoon prints is in soft, wet mud along the banks of rivers, lakes, and streams.

A raccoon uses its front paws quickly and nimbly. It can do just as much with its forepaws as you can with your hands. That includes unscrewing jars, lifting latches, and turning doorknobs. Some raccoons can even untie knots. With such skills, raccoons are able to start all kinds of trouble!

Nifty Movers

Raccoons are not the most graceful animals. They can look awkward and comical as they waddle along on their short legs. However, if they choose to, raccoons can move at great speeds.

If a raccoon gets spooked, it can run as fast as 15 miles (24 km) per hour. That's fast, but it can only manage its top speed for a short distance. It usually heads straight for the safety of the nearest tree.

Raccoons are also pretty good at swimming. They often wade into water in search of food. They also swim across rivers and lakes using the dog-paddle stroke. Once safely on the bank, the raccoon shakes itself energetically to dry its fur.

A raccoon's fur is not waterproof and weighs the animal down as it swims.

A raccoon rests
in a fork of a silver
birch tree.

Agile Climbers

Raccoons are probably most at home in the treetops. These animals are superb climbers thanks to their stout claws and strong, nimble fingers. Their long, bushy tail helps them stay balanced as they run along branches like a squirrel. Many raccoons make their home in trees.

The raccoon rarely slips, but if it does the animal uses its strong claws to hang on as it swings below the branch. The raccoon then clambers along, paw over paw, until it reaches a fork where it can turn the right way up again. When descending, the raccoon does not climb down carefully tail first, like cats and porcupines do. The raccoon can climb down headfirst because it can turn its hind feet sideways to grip the tree trunk.

What's for Supper?

Most types of animals are either plant eaters or meat-eating hunters. A few animals eat both types of foods. Those animals are called **omnivores**, which means "everything eaters." Raccoons are omnivores, along with pigs, bears, and humans.

A raccoon's diet depends on its surroundings. Raccoons that live by water hunt frogs, minnows, turtles, and crayfish. Those that live on coasts search for clams, oysters, and crabs. In other areas, raccoons hunt mice, snakes, snails, insects, and other small creatures.

Raccoons also eat different foods in different seasons. In spring they often steal eggs and baby birds from their nest. In summer they munch on seeds, fruit, and corn, while in fall, acorns, beetles, and other insects are part of their diet. Raccoons eat just about anything they can get their paws on. Their flexible feeding habits help them to thrive in many different places, from cities to the countryside.

Like most other omnivores, raccoons have both sharp teeth for slicing and flat teeth for grinding.

21

Most raccoons search for food at night. They will eat whatever they can find.

Night Raiders

Raccoons are **nocturnal**—they are mainly active at night. When the Sun sets, it's time for them to hunt. They leave their **den** and head for a favorite feeding spot, such as a woodland stream or a line of trash cans in a city suburb. The raccoon wears a little track through the woods or across a backyard as it heads for its usual dining spot.

Not all raccoons are nocturnal. Raccoons that live on the coast adjust their habits to the rhythm of the tides. At low tide, all kinds of creatures get stranded on the shore or trapped in tide pools. Those provide rich pickings for raccoons. For this reason coast-dwelling raccoons hunt at low tide, even if that happens midday.

That's My Patch

Each raccoon has its own home turf, or **territory**.
The size of a territory depends on how much
food there is available. If food is scarce, the
animal needs a large area to gather food. If
the pickings are good, the raccoon's patch can
be much smaller.

Somewhere within its patch is the animal's
den. Raccoons usually make their home inside
hollow trees or caves. They might also move into
an abandoned **burrow** that was dug by another
animal. City raccoons bed down in attics, sheds,
and even garages. Some raccoons have several
dens. Because most of these animals are active at
night, they usually rest by day. They snooze away
the daylight hours until it's time to hunt again.

Up to Mischief

In the days of the Wild West, masked bandits armed with guns used to rob trains and stagecoaches. Raccoons don't have guns, but they do have masks and they do stage robberies! They steal corn from fields and fruit and vegetables from backyards. They are known to raid henhouses for eggs and chickens. One of their favorite tricks is to overturn a trash can, so the contents spill out in the street.

Raccoons get bold if they are hungry. If a raccoon smells something tasty cooking, it may scratch at your door, or bang objects around outside to get your attention. These bandits sometimes enter homes through pet flaps to steal cat and dog food—and they have been known to prey on pets.

If caught in the act, a raccoon can become aggressive. But mostly they work along the lines of: "Don't bother me, and I won't bother you."

A mother raccoon and her young, or kits, relax by the entrance to their den.

Seeing in the Dark

Because humans are active by day, our eyes aren't much use in darkness. But a raccoon's eyes are suited to its nighttime habits.

At the back of the raccoon's eyes is a layer that reflects light. The layer acts like a mirror, reflecting back glimmers of light from the Moon, stars, or even street lamps. That has the effect of adding to whatever light there is. It allows the raccoon to see just as well in darkness as it can in full sunlight.

The reflective layer in a raccoon's eyes also has another effect, which can be quite creepy. If you spot a raccoon at night with the beam of a flashlight, its eyes will shine right back at you with an eerie glow in them!

Hunting at night helps raccoons avoid some enemies, but not all.

Whiskers are sensory hairs that help raccoons find their way around in the dark.

Sharp Senses

Raccoons might see well at night, but they are quite **nearsighted**. That means they can only see well at close range. Also, they cannot see in color. A raccoon's world is black, white, and shades of gray.

Raccoons rely on their good hearing and, especially, their keen sense of smell to locate food. Their ears pick up the sound of a mouse rustling through the grass. Their nose detects the delicious scent of honey in a bees' nest high in a tree.

The raccoon has sensitive whiskers on its snout, which help it find its way even in pitch darkness. The nimble fingers on its front paws are also very sensitive, especially when wet. That allows the raccoon to feel for food such as minnows and crayfish in murky water.

Finger Food

When a raccoon finds food, it might not start to eat immediately. Instead, it often spends time fingering its food and rolling it in its palms. If it is near a stream or pond, it often dunks its food in water. Scientists call this action **dowsing**.

Rather than cleaning its food, scientists think the raccoon is probably enjoying the feel of the food—especially as its paws are super-sensitive when wet. However, raccoons will rinse frogs and toads when they catch them, probably to wash off the nasty-tasting fluid on the skin. As they handle food they might get rid of parts that they cannot eat, such as the stalk of a fruit or the shell of an egg.

A raccoon dowses its
food in a stream in Texas.

Berries are a
favorite food for
raccoons in fall.

Feeding in Fall

Raccoons eat more food in fall than at any other time of year. Northern raccoons can double their weight at this time, as they gorge on seeds, nuts, and berries. One full, contented raccoon captured in fall weighed 62 pounds (28 kg). That's as much as an average eight-year-old child!

Raccoons aren't simply being greedy as they feed in fall—it's how they prepare for winter. They build up a store of thick body fat that will help them last through winter, when the weather is cold and many foods are hard to find.

Raccoons in Winter

In winter raccoons spend a lot of time huddled in their den. In southern areas, the weather is warm enough for them to stay active all winter long. But northern raccoons don't move from their den on freezing winter days.

Raccoons don't truly **hibernate**, as skunks and ground squirrels do. These animals sleep for weeks on end in winter. As they do, their heart rate and breathing slow right down, and they feel cold to the touch. When spring comes they wake up slowly. In contrast, raccoons stay warm and fairly alert, so they can wake up quickly. On mild days they are out and about, looking for food. But when icy winds blow and thick snow covers the ground, they stay put, snug and warm in their nest.

A raccoon interrupts its winter sleep to stretch its legs by an icy stream in Montana.

Male raccoons seek out females in the area surrounding their territory.

38

Be My Mate?

Male raccoons spend much of their life alone. But when the breeding season begins in January or February, they seek a partner. The male wanders through his territory, making loud twittering and chirping sounds to any females within hearing. He might travel up to 8 miles (13 km) each night in search of a **mate**.

If two males come upon a female at the same time, they might fight for the chance to mate with her. However, the strongest male does not always win the female. She chooses the male she wants and the pair shares a den for a couple of weeks. Then the male leaves. He plays no part in bringing up his young. After the male leaves, northern females return to their winter sleep for a few weeks, until warm weather arrives in spring.

Springtime Young

Young raccoons are called **kits**. They are born in April or May, about 65 days after their parents mate. The female gives birth in a nursery den, often in a hollow tree. There are usually four or five young in her **litter**, but raccoon mothers may have up to seven kits.

Newborn raccoons are just 4 inches (10 cm) long and weigh about 2 ounces (60 g). These tiny babies cannot see or hear, because their eyes and ears are sealed. After about ten days their eyes and ears open, but they are still pretty helpless. They spend the first week of their life cuddling up to their mother and drinking her nourishing milk.

A raccoon's milk provides all the nutrients kits need for their first few weeks of life.

41

As raccoon kits get older, they become more adventurous and explore the world outside their den.

Snuggling Up

Newborn kits are covered with fuzzy gray fur. They do not have a mask like their mother—the dark markings appear when they are about ten days old. By this time, the kits are a little more active. As they snuggle up to their mother in a furry bundle, the kit on the outside might get cold. It squirms under its brothers and sisters until it finds a warm spot and takes another nap.

The mother spends all day nursing her babies, and by nightfall she is hungry. She leaves the den in search of food, but races back if she hears her kits crying. If for any reason she feels the nursery is no longer safe, she finds a new den. She then moves her babies to the new site by grabbing each by the scruff of its neck and carrying it in her mouth.

Out into the World

By the time they are two months old, the kits weigh about 4 pounds (2 kg). They have become much more active. Now it is time to leave the den and explore the wider world. This process sometimes starts by accident. A kit leans too far out of the den and takes a tumble! It usually lands on the ground safe and sound— but very surprised.

Kits usually begin exploring in the company of their mother. They follow in a furry line as she climbs down the tree and moves about her territory. If danger threatens, the mother draws her babies around her. Raccoons are so fierce and fearless that most **predators** think twice about attacking them. But a kit on its own would make an easy target. Fortunately for the young raccoons, few animals fight as fiercely as a raccoon mother defending her young!

A mother raccoon keeps a careful eye on her kit.

Young raccoons practice their climbing skills.

46

New Experiences

On outings with their mother, the kits start to sample other foods besides her milk. They try seeds, grass, and berries. They watch as the mother catches tadpoles and crickets, and then try to follow her example. At first, the kits don't have much luck with hunting, but practice makes perfect. With all those new foods to sample, young raccoons grow quickly, putting on about 2 pounds (1 kg) in a month.

Like most young animals, kits love to play. The best fun is a game of tag with their brothers and sisters. They also hold wrestling matches, pouncing on and pretending to bite one another. If their mother thinks the game is getting too rough, she growls a warning. Play-fighting teaches the kits to hunt and defend themselves—important lessons for life.

Bold and Curious

By late summer the kits have become bold and daring. They still go with their mother on hunting trips, but now they forge ahead or linger behind to investigate nooks and crannies. Being naturally curious, the kits sometimes get into trouble, but their mother is usually there to help them. Eventually they go hunting without her, either in the company of a brother or sister, or on their own.

By fall, the kits are as big as their mother. They now find all their own food, but usually stay with their mother through their first winter. The following spring, they strike out on their own, as their mother prepares to have a new litter. Each young raccoon wanders off to find its own feeding territory. It won't be long before they are starting their own family. With luck, raccoons live for up to 12 years in the wild and have many litters of young.

Words to Know

Burrow   The underground home of an
                  animal, such as a fox or badger.

Camouflage   The colors and markings on an
                  animal that help it blend in with
                  its surroundings.

Carnivores   Mammals that mostly eat meat.
                  Carnivores include cats, dogs,
                  weasels, and raccoons.

Den   The home of an animal.

Dowsing   When a raccoon dips its food in water.

Guard hairs   The long, silky hairs that form the
                  outer layer of a raccoon's fur coat.

Hibernate   To enter a deep sleeplike state
                  in order to survive winter.

Kits   Young raccoons.

Litter	A group of young born to a mother at the same time.
Mammals	Animals with hair on their body that feed their young with milk.
Mate	Either of a pair of breeding animals; to come together to produce young.
Nearsighted	Able to see well only at close range.
Nocturnal	Of an animal that is active at night.
Omnivores	Animals that eat both plants and animals.
Predators	Animals that hunt other animals.
Species	The scientific word for animals of the same type that can breed together.
Territory	The area where an animal lives, hunts, and breeds, and which it defends against others of its kind.

Find Out More

Books

Baglio, B. M. *Raccoons on the Roof*. Animal Ark.
New York: Scholastic, Inc, 2001.

Kite, L. P. *Raccoons*. Early Bird Nature Books.
Minneapolis, Minnesota: Lerner Publishing Group,
2003.

Web sites

Raccoon
*www.enchantedlearning.com/subjects/mammals/raccoon/
Raccoonprintout.shtml*
Facts about raccoons and a picture to print.

Raccoon (Procyon lotor)
*animals.nationalgeographic.com/animals/mammals/
raccoon.html*
Information about raccoons.

Index